POETRY
*now*

# *THE PATH OF LIFE*

Edited by

Andrew Head

First published in Great Britain in 1998 by
*POETRY NOW*
1-2 Wainman Road, Woodston,
Peterborough, PE2 7BU
Telephone (01733) 230746
Fax (01733) 230751



HB ISBN 1 86188 636 5
SB ISBN 1 86188 631 4

# *FOREWORD*

Although we are a nation of poetry writers we are accused of not reading poetry and not buying poetry books: after many years of listening to the incessant gripes of poetry publishers, I can only assume that the books they publish, in general, are books that most people do not want to read.

Poetry should not be obscure, introverted, and as cryptic as a crossword puzzle: it is the poet's duty to reach out and embrace the world.

The world owes the poet nothing and we should not be expected to dig and delve into a rambling discourse searching for some inner meaning.

The reason we write poetry (and almost all of us do) is because we want to communicate: an ideal; an idea; or a specific feeling. Poetry is as essential in communication, as a letter; a radio; a telephone, and the main criteria for selecting the poems in this anthology is very simple: they communicate.

The Path of Life is an anthology we can all read and many will seem to have a very personal feeling for each of us.

This is a general book discussing issues from anything such as a favourite holiday, to as far afield as the millennium and a special wish.

Whilst reading this anthology we can gain a small insight into the important aspects of the poet's life, how similar are they to you?

# *CONTENTS*


| | | |
|---|---|---|
| One Wish | Don Goodwin | 1 |
| Kastaroni Bay | Sylvia Hopwood | 2 |
| A Ventnorian's View Of The Joys Of Learning . . . | Wilfred John Parker | 3 |
| Surplus To Requirements | Jay Baker | 5 |
| Me | Constance M Smith | 6 |
| The Silence Of Grief | Rosamund Husdon | 7 |
| This Son Of Mine? | Nick Rogers | 8 |
| Spring In The Air | Sybellena Bridge | 9 |
| Images In The Clouds | Carol Rees | 10 |
| In Memory | K F Adamson | 11 |
| Untitled | David Trump | 12 |
| Together | Jill Davies | 13 |
| Red Balloon | Alison Thrower | 14 |
| Untitled | Marilyn Hayne | 15 |
| You And I Together, Forever | Daniel Brooks | 16 |
| Kate's Phone Call, Christmas 1997 | J S Liberkowski | 17 |
| Water | Brian Cunningham | 18 |
| Life | Adam Coren | 19 |
| You | Peter Koessler | 20 |
| New Life | Steve Thorne | 21 |
| Donna | Marjorie Edwina Ashley | 22 |
| Remembering Sandy | Irene Gunnion | 23 |
| Exercise Is Good For You! | P M Tarbatt | 25 |
| Deaf | Doreen Jones | 26 |
| A Party Of One | J W Parker | 27 |
| Hideaway | C Geldard | 29 |
| Drained | Caroline Tully | 30 |
| My First And Only Love | Nancy Bell | 31 |
| The Night Watchman | J Ball | 32 |
| The Struggle | Val McDermid | 33 |
| The Killing Season | Pauline Skipworth | 34 |
| From Dusk To Dawn | Nora M Kirienko | 35 |
| Trees | Anne C Richmond | 36 |
| When We Marry | N S Howells | 37 |

| | | |
|---|---|---|
| Visits Abroad | Nicholas Redshaw | 38 |
| Smiles | Andrew Mountford Jones | 39 |
| The Thaw | David Francis Jones | 40 |
| Silent Is The Station | Beryl Mountford Jones | 41 |
| The Twelve Months Of Life | Carol Griffiths | 42 |
| The Last Of The Brave | David Wasley | 43 |
| Conversational Piece | Carole M Pickworth | 44 |
| Raging Seas | Marion Pollitt | 45 |
| The Old Barn | Lois Ounssi | 46 |
| Reflection | Adam Davis | 47 |
| View From A Wheelchair | Marion Holt | 48 |
| Summer Sun And Cat | Ged M Bretherton | 49 |
| The Waste | P T Swayne | 50 |
| It's The Holidays | Tricia Gerrish | 51 |
| Golden Trumpets | Joan Smith | 52 |
| Restless Night | Isabel Murray | 53 |
| Innocent Within | Karen Henderson | 54 |
| The Love Child | Alison Birch | 55 |
| What A Wonderful Feeling | Kirsty Louise Penfold | 56 |
| Hurt | Karla Jaggers | 57 |
| Grace | Claire Shrewsbury | 58 |
| Before I Die | Denis Joseph | 59 |
| My Wish For Mankind In A Troubled World | Maureen Joy Lynch | 61 |
| Treasured Memories | A Langley | 62 |
| Victory | D H Reasbeck | 63 |
| Delights Of Yorkshire | Andrew Dickson | 64 |
| Melika | Suzan Gumush | 66 |
| The Shadow | W W Lund | 67 |
| Strongest | Patrick Miller | 68 |
| The Park | Clare Whitaker | 69 |
| Summer | Pauline Burton | 70 |
| Confined Optimism | Emma Scott-Smith | 71 |
| Query To A Friend | Lee Spencer | 72 |
| Flames | P Morrill | 73 |
| Thoughts And Dreams | Margaret J Robinson | 74 |
| I'm Sure Tadpoles Bite | John A Marsden | 75 |
| Recollection | A D Tarr | 76 |

| | | |
|---|---|---|
| Never To Know A Moment Of Loneliness | Saiqa Parveen | 77 |
| Unsure | Barry Taylor | 78 |
| A Place For Me | Amanda Keighley | 79 |
| Special Woman | Jonathan Bryant | 80 |
| A Winter's Night | Carole Morris | 81 |
| Mother | Alison Head | 82 |
| Time | Helen S Newey | 84 |
| Isn't It A Lovely Day | Rowena O'Mahony | 85 |
| Biscuit Blues | Michelle Power | 86 |
| Changing Times | Frances Kennedy | 87 |
| The Battle | Rachel Angus | 88 |
| Costumes and Scenery | S Whitehead | 89 |
| Wind Whispers | Betty Tindal | 90 |
| King Of Rings | Ann Copland | 91 |
| Tomorrow | Julia Ann Davis | 92 |
| Smile | Douglas Bonthron | 93 |
| Golbal Warning | Margery English | 94 |
| Winter Time | Lynne Heather West | 95 |
| Emily Jane | Shaun Hillen | 96 |
| The Visit | V Magrs | 97 |
| The Neighbours From Hell | S A Buckingham | 98 |
| Cyril VC | Richard Beeson | 99 |
| Keep Smiling | B Phillips | 101 |
| Titanic | Alan Jones | 102 |
| The Dead Poet | Amanda Hillbeck | 103 |
| An Educated Scarecrow | K J Herbert | 104 |
| Taking Time To Care | Mandy Jayne Moon | 105 |
| Summer Of '41 | P W Spencer | 106 |
| Why Don't My Children Love Me | Janet Brown | 107 |
| Modern Medicine | Helen Cronin | 108 |
| Growing Pains | Veronica Black | 109 |
| An Englishman's Home | Kim Montia | 110 |
| Sometimes | Stephanie Bones | 111 |
| Poem For A Princess | Laura Sage | 112 |
| Bill | F E Cove | 113 |
| Diana | Anne Scrimshaw | 114 |

| | | |
|---|---|---|
| Beauty - To Paint | Lydia Barnett | 115 |
| Following Your Dreams | Danielle Turner | 116 |
| Love | Rachel Johnston | 117 |
| Reasons | M M Kirkham | 119 |
| Firemoon | Stuart A Brown | 120 |
| On Glancing Through A Holiday Guide | Eileen Bales | 121 |
| God's Family | Emily Hodson | 122 |
| I Wish | M Wakefield | 123 |
| Spring | M Tickle | 124 |
| Growing Old | Edith Buckeridge | 125 |
| Snow In Scotland | Kenneth Mood | 126 |
| Heaven Called For Our Angel | Brian Marshall | 127 |
| Past And Present | Ivy Cawood | 128 |
| For Armistice Sunday | Douglas Peet | 129 |
| Island Of Dreams | J F Grainger | 130 |
| Life In The Year 9791 | H G Griffiths | 131 |
| Limited Edition | Bakewell Burt | 132 |
| The Truck Stop 2000 | Donald Jay | 133 |
| Hump Phery | James R B McCurdie | 134 |
| Imaginary Friend | GIG | 135 |
| Sensations | Gail Susan Halstead | 136 |
| True Friends | Timothy Webster | 137 |
| Wind | D J Blackburn | 138 |
| Thoughts Of You | Mia Ryan | 139 |

## One Wish

Someone asked me if I had one wish,
Would it be for some succulent dish.
Would it be for wealth uncountable,
Or for fame that was unsamoutable.
If I had one wish then it would be,
That everyone could see Jesus just like me.
And that he'd have a place within their hearts,
Before it is too late and He does depart.

***Don Goodwin***

## KASTARONI BAY

There is a place where you can stay,
A remote and peaceful bay.
Watch the fishing boats bob and sway,
Where people live life in a different way.
A simple life of carefree days,
Where all your worries drift away,
Like the tide, it ebbs and wave,
Never really here to stay.
Hot sunbeams come dance on me,
Reflecting on a deep blue sea,
Pebbles formed perfect round, colours of many kind,
A place to restore the mind
A freedom of a different kind.

***Sylvia Hopwood***

## A Ventnorian's View Of The Joys Of Learning To Sail In Beautiful Ventnor-Bay

Come down to beautiful Ventnor Bay
where water-sportsmen safely play.
Fanned by a gentle on-shore breeze,
even novice sailors feel at ease.

Young sailors can their mistakes make
ashore, at the model boating lake,
by the Cascade, on Eastern Esplanade,
where model yachts can safely cannonade.

As sailors learn their skills so swiftly
their models start to move quite quickly.
As winds veer, and back, each quarter
their yachts change direction on the water.

At last, the fundamentals learned,
young sailors watch the sails being furled.
Then, down to the full-size boats ashore,
to learn safe-sailing skills galore.

Then, with life-jackets on, they trail
to their own sailing-dinghy, for their first sail.
At last, they are safely on the water,
for experiences which they soon will master.

With an instructor to help them 'learn the ropes',
they learn to avoid the other boats,
and soon, the young sailors, without delay,
can themselves sail their boats across the Bay.

Then, as the sun sinks in the west,
each comes ashore to do his best
to furl the sail, and beach his boat,
contented, with his life afloat.

Help is at hand for remaining queries,
as instructors teach them the latest theories.
Young sailors can then enjoy every day
within our glorious Ventnor Bay.

***Wilfred John Parker***

## SURPLUS TO REQUIREMENTS

Once upon a time I belonged. I found a niche
Where there was happiness and was needed.
Never would I consider trading to be rich
Now I know I am surplus to requirements.

Each job . . . wife, homemaker, mother and lover
Are these I did with head held high, with every ounce of my being.
Now I live constantly wondering what I have done to suffer,
To become simply surplus to requirement.

No encircling arms or male stalwart
To understand the tears and tears I have cried,
To ensure my family would never disaster court,
Just to become surplus to requirements.

They have flown the coop after spreading their wings,
Successfully glided on the thermals of delight.
I have done my best to overcome problems life brings,
Only to observe I am surplus to requirements.

Ill heath has clipped my wings, now never to fly.
I am totally dependent, when I expected to be free.
I wonder is there anyone there to hear my dismal cry,
Because I am simply surplus to requirements.

***Jay Baker***

## Me

I look in the mirror and what do I see?
An elderly woman . . . can it really be me.
When did all those wrinkles appear on my face
And those once so firm contours
Disappear without trace.
My grey hairs I can hide with the help of a tint,
But these old legs no longer care much for a sprint . . .
And over the years I am sad to relate
That my waist line has grown to one score and eight.
My other statistics just don't bear a mention . . .
Whilst to corns and calluses
I must now give attention.
Though my teeth are quite pearly they are not my own,
And it's hard to believe I was once seven stone . . .
But when I retire for the night
And shut my bedroom door
The years fade away and I'm sixteen once more.

***Constance M Smith***

## THE SILENCE OF GRIEF

I crouch beneath the old oak tree
Eyes filled with deepening pain
Tears fall in silent empathy
With the early morning rain
Against thick bark I press my brow
To calm my sorrowing mind
My safe and trusted confidant
Offering strength and care combined
The rustling trees bring solace
As the grief and anger flow
No words of love are needed
Just the peace lone woodlands show
I rest my aching body
Where carpets of green fern
Gently spread the warmth of hope
As sad, cold thoughts return
In time a hint of sunshine
Through mists of finest white
As my crying heart is eased
And caressed by soothing light.

***Rosamund Hudson***

## This Son Of Mine?

So what was he like,
This son I never had.
Was he like his mum,
Or like his dad?

Did his smile beam,
All bright and gay?
This little mite
Who never saw the light of day.

He was more than a twinkle,
And more than a bump,
But less than a life
Held close in my arms.

Why was he thrust
Into a world so stark.
To see nothing of life,
Only the dark.

***Nick Rogers***

## Spring In The Air

Springtime a time of hope for
    Those in deep despair
A time for love to come along
    To find someone who cares
The green buds are appearing
    Upon the black thorn bush
Snowdrops are standing tearful
    Crocuses in quick pursuit
The little lambs are frolicking
    O'er the daisies' struggling heads
Children in the school playground
    Their voices echoes all around
But all too soon spring will have gone
    And summer will be here
And I shall sit and ponder
    On what spring will bring next year.

***Sybellena Bridge***

## Images In The Clouds

Angels gathering in the clouds,
Laden in their long white shrouds.
A little angel appears in the light,
Then there is darkness and she's gone out of sight.
I wish I could see her angelic face again,
I'd love to see her smile.
I wonder where she came from,
Could she have been mine.

I want to hold her hand, but she's fading away,
If only for a little while she was allowed to stay.
Cats, dogs, horses and sheep,
If only these images I could keep.
Unicorns, dolls and teddy bears,
And roundabout rides you see at fairs.
Mermaids, witches, planes and trains,
And there's an umbrella in case it rains.

A guitar, a settee, and a chair,
A banana, an apple and a pear.
A dragon, a leaf and a flying kite,
And in the mist a motor bike.
All these images are there to see,
You could see them just like me.
Look up at the clouds above,
And you might even see the one you love.

***Carol Rees***

## In Memory

I awaken at the first break of morning light
    that chases moon and stars in daily flight
I see the dawn trap a blossom's new day smile
    and witnessing this I hesitate awhile!

I blink as the sun causes my staring to yield
    in pensive mood I turn to cross the field
sighing as the summer day awakens old desires
    of a love in my heart time never expires!

In the field stood an isolated blossom tree
    on sentry there a small bird I could see
within the confines of branches gently blown
    rehearsing notes till its song had grown!

Then the nightingale sang to a budding rose
    asking if this is where all beauty grows
the flower blushed red upon its tender cheek
    as did my love when I dared first speak!

Within the rhythmic beat of the bird's melodies
    lingering in the music, haunting memories
in the freshness of the garden blooming there
    the scent of the red rose upon her hair!

Now there is something here that I must reveal
    that from the tree a blossom I did steal
the nightingale sat on guard yet can't bemoan
    a single red rose for my love's headstone!

***K F Adamson***

## Untitled

*(Written in the Maldives on holiday with my son Zachary - early morning late November '97)*

On reflection I arrived to this white humid atoll a lonely person
Vexed for the love of a good woman and being disappointed when
settling stirs
My guilt overwhelms me, guardian angels have not addressed
my unconscious mind
I believe in celestial reckonings but refused to live the modern ways
Self trust like well washed garments, loved but tried of purpose.
The gold rush started long ago but didn't stop at the mountains.
Men are getting selfish and focus on other icons.
Ways of the spear give way to comfort drinking and heavy frames.
Ideals are traded for Judas tokens, profit at any cost.
Bringing my son to this atoll will give me time to talk with his
young soul.
Growing fast, buds with few leaves are concerned with his
position in the window
Meditation, reflection and a willingness in self belief is our
chartered course.
It is a confusing time for him, hormones pounding and bill boards
on a foggy day.
Which direction is it, upside down, where am I, my son needs
to know - so hence the trip.

***David Trump***

## TOGETHER

When first you are married, your life is a dream,
Your man is attentive, trustworthy, clean.
He'll do any task just to please his new bride,
He'll walk tall and proud with his wife by his side.

When you tell him you're pregnant he'll help all he can,
You've made him so proud, you've proved him a man.
He'll pamper and spoil you, you'll feel like a queen,
He's the happiest guy that you ever have seen.

Several years have gone by since you walked down the aisle,
Two more children arrived and time's faded your smile.
You're always exhausted, he's always tired too,
There's just not enough time for the things you should do.

With the kids in their teens now the money is short,
All the clothes and the shoes and the food must be bought.
Tempers get frayed when you can't make ends meet,
There's no money for extras, you can't spoil him with treats.

Middle age comes along and once more you're alone,
The children have gone from the once hectic home.
You begin to remember the life you once had,
With your caring, attentive and handsome young lad.

When old age finally hits you you're happy with life,
You've spent many good years being that once *young lad's* wife.
Your children are busy with kids of their own,
You're contented and happy to be all alone.

So when God finally calls you to answer,
If he asks 'What's been good in your life?'
You'll look back through the years and tell him,
'I spent wonderful years as his wife.'

***Jill Davies***

## Red Balloon

Green, speed blurred grass passes your eyes,
Behind on string red balloon flies.
Laughing you turn, waving to me,
But fall to cry as string goes free.
Small hands empty, face to the sky,
Weeping when eyes see red float by.

What reason is there for your tears?
A lost toy or more worldly cares,
That you are a captive of ground
Never to fly, gravity bound?

Long to escape, to float and dance
With passing breeze, I'd take my chance
To mock gravity, cut my strings
And so, triumphant, be of wings.

***Alison Thrower***

## Untitled

Where was my love, my share of comfort?
Likened to a creature below a stone
Alive - an essential part of life's circle
Barely noticed, soon forgotten, feeling desperately alone.

You have your place but do not hinder
Appear and be scorched, destroyed, put down.
You are not welcome, out here with us
You don't belong, keep your distance they frown.

You knew I was there, but I had no value
I irritated, or became a pest
What was it in me, that you so hated?
What part of me did you detest?

Perhaps, like the ant, I have strength and power
For one so small, I can achieve
And just by doing, be of worth and wonder
The chrysalis its old skin, will struggling leave.

And all the material that rots to the earth
Will no longer matter from whence it came
For I will travel and tread upon it
To make my home and triumph claim.

Each step and challenge, uphill I take
Each morsel of rubbish, I chew and spit out
Will build a mound that will become my mountain
And upon it I will stand proud and shout
*'I made it, I matter'*
And that my fellow creatures, is what it's all about.

***Marilyn Hayne***

## YOU AND I TOGETHER, FOREVER

I feel lost without you by my side,
So with my time I must abide,
With the rules of my love for you.
My love for you could never be blue
And to you I remain forever true,
So tell me that you feel the same,
For two it takes to play this game.
My feelings for you, are love so high,
Accompanied by a moonlit sky.
Please I pray, feel the same as I,
Because my love for you
Is here to stay,
Beyond the day, the day
I die.

***Daniel Brooks***

## KATE'S PHONE CALL, CHRISTMAS 1997

I hear your voice over the telephone,
'It's me,' you say . . . but, I recognised,
Time stops,
Time stops . . . I want to cry,
I look for hidden reasons . . . then, I wonder why
I freeze, so vulnerable here . . .
So all alone.
Are you playing games or are you just a friend,
Did the past for you, like me, never go away,
Or is there something,
Or is there something . . . that you need to say.
Do you, think of me . . . do you hope and pray,
To mend the hurt that came,
Sadly before the end.
I used to laugh about a broken heart,
But there is no joy for me now I know so much pain,
If only,
If only . . . I could hold you close to me again,
And feel your love repair,
A broken heart.

***J S Liberkowski***

## WATER

‘Water, water everywhere’ and so the old line goes,
But no-one ever seems to ask to where *that* water flows?
Perhaps it flows down to the sea, across a rolling land,
Through wondrous landscapes, it would seem,
Carved by a giant’s hand?
Or perhaps it flows up to a shore
Where magic beasts do roam,
And children play for ever more
In gardens they call home?
Or perhaps it flows up to a mountain lake,
Where silver fishes glide,
And kisses once upon the shore
In some moon’s golden tide?
Do sailing boats divide it twain,
Upon a Summer’s day,
Or founder on the Rocks of Life
Along its winding way?

Mayhap we will never truly know
To where that water goes,
But hope that all our waking dreams
In *that* pure water flows.

To see the places never seen,
Where’er the water goes.
That is my wish, and my dream . . .
To know what no-one knows.

***Brian Cunningham***

## Life

People staring
People looking down
High and low
They're all around
Laughing and sniggering at your expense
Never to think about your distress

Never a thought they have for you
Destroying everything you used to do
Feelings you have and feelings you knew
So far apart
It couldn't be you

Taking your dreams and throwing them down
Sitting like a god in their golden crown
Making you what they want you to be
They'll take control of your destiny

They'll chew you up and spit you out
Leaving you hopeless
You can't work it out
Your brain's like a jungle
Can't find your way through
All in a mess
Trying to be you

All they want is what you give
Never returning any of your gifts
A feeling so deep, so deep down low
A feeling of losing complete control
Where are you going
Where have you been
What do you know,
What have you seen
Confidence gone, no control
Taken from you by those who don't know

***Adam Coren***

## You

Your love was sent from heaven
To me on the wings of a dove,
All I can give you in return
Is my true and everlasting love.

You mean everything to me
You set my world afire,
I think of you constantly
You are my one desire.

And if you say you'll love me too
Everything will be so sweet,
I'll work hard to make life good for you
And my life will be complete.

To have your love for evermore
And to hold you in my arms,
I'll devote myself to loving you
In the wonder of your charms.

***Peter Koessler***

## New Life

In our home there's now a new life,
It's nice to have the trouble and strife,
Into everything learning things new,
Once he's seen you'd love him too,
Although at night he'll cry and yell,
Only to hear 'Go sleep' we tell,
There's no doubt he's tiring stuff,
Is our new puppy who we call Scruff.

***Steve Thorne***

## DONNA

You have the most beautiful face,
A smile so tender and full of grace
Your eyes are bright, and always alert
When friends are near, you're the extrovert.
You welcome me, stand and guide,
Your mistress by your side.
You understand our language, but don't speak,
Words are unnecessary, you have better technique.
You're full of love with a golden heart,
As a guide dog you've played your part.
Now you're retired after your guiding career,
Have a good rest, and enjoy your golden years.

***Marjorie Edwina Ashley***

## REMEMBERING SANDY
*(Adored pet - sadly missed)*

It was our island
How I remember
It so well
Where dandling trees
Housed ring dove sweet
'Twas our own
Magic - wooded dell
Fallen branches - that oft'
We hopped skipped through
In days of laughter
Endless song
It was our island
Yes - it was
For there
We both belonged.

Demure snowdrop
Flowered in early spring
With heartsease
Pleased to greet
I remember,
Sandy
Yes - I do!
Our favourite spot
And picnic seat.

Memorable moments
All but left
For me
Friend and companion
Now you've gone
But hush - my tears - in
Remembering
That in our island
You still roam.

***Irene Gunnion***

## EXERCISE IS GOOD FOR YOU!

Oh please, oh please may this end soon.
I offer up a silent prayer, whilst spinning round the room.
'Now step one and two and three and four,
Then begin your exercises on the floor.'

I take a second to glance around,
Everyone else looks refreshingly sound,
Make-up perfect, bodies trim,
Pulsating with energy right up to the brim.

I toss my damp hair from out of my eyes,
Fat must be going from off my thighs!
Mascara is running down my cheek,
I've to do it all again next week.

'Thank you ladies that's all for today'
What was that I heard her say?
Oh joy, oh joy for now that's it,
There's nothing to it this keeping fit.

The ladies depart, laughing and gay,
Smelling as sweet as new mown hay.
Whilst I feel like a very damp squid,
Can't believe this cost me sixteen quid!

***P M Tarbatt***

## DEAF

Have you ever thought what life would be like
If you'd never heard your name,
If the sounds of day, and still of night
To you were just the same?

If you never heard the doorbell ring
Or the miaowing of the cat
Have you really ever stopped to think
What life would be like that?

Never to hear the bark of a dog
Or the voice of a loved one dear,
The songs of the birds in early spring
That tell us summer's near.

To treat the deaf ones gently
Have patience with them too,
Say a little prayer for them
And be thankful it's not you.

***Doreen Jones***

## A Party Of One

A forgotten Christmas was held this year, in a run down
rambling home,
Held for a ticking of a clock, and an old lady who lives
alone.
A party for those many lost years, for the family long past,
and gone,
And in her best room she will sip her tea, kept special for
so long.
No-one responds to her plaintive call, or answers when
she speaks,
The only sounds to fall upon her ears, are creaking doors
and squeaks.
The silent vows, married to her past, be-seated quiet within
her room,
She awaits the final curtain-call, when heavenly light will flood
her gloom.
Many years passed in solitude, and living by her stealth,
Finding that loneliness was no friend, when living by herself.
In days, she died, whilst fast asleep, within the dusking of
her room,
No-one called in, and no-one knew, she had escaped her
silent tomb.
Now a grave lies apart from the rest, marked with one solitary
stone,
Way back beyond the stand of yew and oak, this grave now
stands alone.
This place soon to overgrow from neglect, wrote down in life
and willed,
Lies the aged body of a lonely soul, whose last wish was duly
filled.
The statement made on her demise, was simple and concise,
Bury me where I'll be forgot, far away from prying eyes.
For in life folk passed her by, never enquiring how she was,
No consideration for her well-being, which left her at a loss.

And so in death, be as in life, though not her wish, she'd state,
Leave me lonely and unloved, leave me to my fate.
Now many years have passed, her wish still holds true today,
The gravestone long neglected now, in time did flake away.
So now no mark can be gleaned from that crumbling stone,
Which holds the fate of all of us, who find ourselves alone.

***J W Parker***

## Hideaway

Inside of me there's a secret place
Where no-one knows
Where no-one goes
For it's desolate
A place to mourn
Of dreams unborn
Of hopes unreached
A lost belief.

A realm of dreams
Still locked, still leashed
Unpursued and left
To lie dormant.

***C Geldard***

## DRAINED

My brain is drained of thoughts
my heart of love
my shell of beauty
my eyes of joy
my lips of smiles
my soul of hope.

***Caroline Tully***

## My First And Only Love

Aged twenty-one and very naive
My first love I did perceive.
Twenty years my senior and very self-assured,
For a number of years, I secretly adored.
Eventually, I secretly sent
This Valentine. Sincerely meant.

You my dear man, I always find
Are honest, decent, clean and kind.
You respect yourself and others too,
I really do *admire you.*
With your nicely tanned skin and eyes so blue.
My heart's desire, I love you.
Happy together we could be
Until the call to eternity.
Though family commitments keep us apart
Now and forever, you hold my heart.

The years passed by, we did not marry.
It is a sad mistake to love and then tarry.
Now, sad to say, he is dead and gone
And I am left to carry on.

***Nancy Bell***

## The Night Watchman

I know he watches, I feel no fear,
without invitation he will appear.
He'll sometimes hide, I know he's there,
but where exactly I couldn't swear.
He'll watch you through the night-time,
and sometimes in the day,
But best caught in the darkness,
when rain clouds stand at bay.
His smiling face will warm your heart,
he comforts lonely souls,
He's mentioned in all ghostly tales,
and most romantic roles.
To bathe within his loving light,
something we all have done,
To watch him in the harvest-time,
glowing gold just like a sun.
His longest watch he's made till now,
began before mankind,
To radiate his lunar light as long as he can shine.
So when you look above your heads,
and search the starlight sky,
remember the night-watchman,
he shines for you and I.

***J Ball***

## The Struggle

They tell us and advise us
Keep healthy and live longer
Eat wisely and grow stronger
Stay slim and keep in trim
Even do a jog in the gym
We're told not to smoke
To give up is a joke
Tell us, just how do we cope?

'Here's what to do, to keep in step
Willpower you need to keep in check
First of all, select a day
Join a club and pave the way
Stick to the rules, go on a diet
Do not give up, you have to try it
Another rule, that also applies
Of course, it is plenty of exercise
Use your legs, instead of the car
In the end, it won't seem far
The calories reduced, your next battle,
Smoking is out, be ready to tackle
At first cut down by one or two
The rest is now left up to you.'

It's hard we know, to adhere to the rule
If you do, you'll be no fool!
A better person you will be
Time will tell, just wait and see.

***Val McDermid***

## The Killing Season

I bob my head through a hole in the ice,
Frolicking about, the water seems nice,
I am a seal, that lives in the sea,
I fear no-one and no-one fears me.

I knew no worries about human life,
Of family troubles, stress or strife,
Until my world of tranquillity,
Was invaded by man, on a killing spree.

All around is pure and white,
But something red is staining the ice,
It's the blood of seals, *young and old,*
Being murdered, for their skins to be sold.

There's no compassion in the face above,
Devoid of all pity, guilt or love,
I plead with my eyes, it's a futile cry,
I know that I am soon to die.

The air hangs heavy with the scent of death,
As the weapon is lifted to batter my head,
Pain, blackness, then nothing at all,
One seal less, next spring, when the
Grim Reaper calls.

***Pauline Skipworth***

## FROM DUSK TO DAWN

Twilight subdued the dying day
Until night took that, too, away.
Then darkness held the night in thrall,
And not a sound was heard at all.
Towards the dawn, a gentle breeze
Arose, and shook the sleeping trees,
Until the leaves fell to the ground,
And from the undergrowth around
With silent footsteps came the day
And swept the shades of night away.

*Nora M Kirienko*

## TREES

Bronze, gold and deepest red I see
My heart overflows with love for the tree:
Whilst all around me progress creeps, the tree its stately fashion keeps.

The seasons come - the seasons go,
Its branches bared in winter snow,
Then fertile spring its barren boughs will kiss and pregnant buds
await the summer bliss.

All beauty surrounds in masses of green,
High summer is here a joy to be seen.
The forest, the glade, the hedgerow too are heavy in leaf all shiny
and new.

The sun's heat rays and gentle summer rain
Caress the leaves and turn them gold again,
Another autumn preceding the cold but still the colours are varied
and bold.

***Anne C Richmond***

## When We Marry

When I meet you at the altar
Will you hold my hand so tight
So I'll have no inhibitions
And confirm I'm doing right

Can I lean upon your shoulder
When I feel I want to cry
Will you tell me words of comfort
And wipe the tears from my eye

Will you embrace me and console me
When trouble comes our way
Feed me scraps of confirmation
And drive all my fears away

Give me happiness and pleasure
To do the things we said we'd do
So we'll always have the memories
We can once again renew

If we ever have a quarrel
And at each other shout
Will you whisper that you love me
Before the light goes out

Let me feel your warmth and passion
As we touch each other's hand
Let the feeling last forever
As I yield to your command

If you do these things I ask you
Then you never will regret
For I will on my honour
Be the best wife you can get.

***N S Howells***

## Visits Abroad

I think I'd rather have followed me father.
He worked on a farm, it did him no harm.
I'd be there too if it wasn't for you.
But you wanted things we couldn't afford,
like patio doors and visits abroad.

So I put on a shirt and went off to work.
The shirt's white collar makes it harder to swalla'.
My trousers pressed I look me best.
I sit in a chair, next to him over there.
Sitting all day, tapping away.
I alter the bits in silicon chips.
I process the words and have you heard,
the noise in me brain, I'm going insane.
'Cos you wanted things we couldn't afford,
like patio doors and visits abroad.

I drive all day, to hear them say,
'It all went wrong at half past one'
and 'Where were you?' and 'What should we do?'
The biscuits I eat, they rot me teeth.
Burgers for dinner, but I'm getting thinner.
What BSE? It won't happen to me.
I'm tired all day, all work no play.
Can't sleep at night, try as I might.
I wake in the morning still tired and yawning.
'Cos you wanted things we couldn't afford,
like patio doors and visits abroad.

But I get paid well for what we sell.
I can't complain, I'm using me brain.
So I'll tap away to earn me pay,
To buy patio doors; visits abroad;
and all those things that we can't afford!

***Nicholas Redshaw***

## Smiles

Smiles,
Reminiscent of good times,
No longer prominent.
View is clouded,
Rain is permanent.
Jokes and laughter
Long experienced,
But cherished deep
And not forgotten.
How I long for those times to reappear,
For life to be fun,
To be without fear.

Smiles,
Signs of contentment.
But I am without them,
Desiring much
But feeling unfit
To withstand oncoming pressures.
People relying on me
And I can't take it.
I need to straighten my life
First and foremost.

Smiles come back.

***Andrew Mountford Jones***

## The Thaw

Snow-capped mountains cold and bleak
Way too high for goats or sheep,
Await the spring.
For the expected thaw when down to the valley
The melt will pour.
Rills, runnels, rivulets cascade
Not stopped by dam, dyke or barricade.
Cold water enters the valley stream
Enlivening the trout of the angler's dream.
Meandering along through gorse and heather
Tinkling and bubbling, light as a feather.
Along many a mile of lush green meadow,
To gently greet the river where oarsmen row.
Now the water is slow and deep,
Whilst silent beneath its mud
Bream, tench and carp do sleep.
The water appears so slow and cold,
But the volume increases a thousand fold.
Down to its estuary on a circuitous route,
Over the tidal pan like a muddy soup,
In a myriad of channels the waters hide,
Then all do vanish to an incoming tide.

***David Francis Jones***

## Silent Is The Station

Sandstone walls black with the soot
And grime of countless years,
Silent sentinels,
Tower above the grey deserted platforms.
Platforms empty, where once an army of cloth
Capped men erupted from the crowded trains,
The tramp, tramp tramping of their steel shod boots
Echoing down the cold dark tunnels.

Silent is the station,
No rush hour stream of muffler wrapped
Woodbine smoking men,
Thronging the platforms end to end,
Only a trickle of passengers,
Stand,
Separate.
Soon gone,
Silent is the station.

***Beryl Mountford Jones***

## THE TWELVE MONTHS OF LIFE

Happy New Year, January arrives
What changes are coming to affect our lives.
The sales are on, the weather gets worse
February sees an empty purse.

Valentine's Day, love in the air
Holidays picked from the armchair.
Here comes March, watch those winds
Hard to keep on your pins.

April dawns, spring is here
Easter eggs bring a cheer.
The month of May comes so bright
Longer days and shorter nights.

Saving's ended, holidays start
June warms up everyone's heart.
A sunny morn brings July
Barbecue days you can rely.

Lovely gardens with flowers in bloom
Giving August plenty of room.
Bank holiday comes and goes with flare
September sees the trees are bare.

Autumn starts, October's in
Hallowe'en brings marked pumpkins.
November 5th, it's Guy Fawkes' night
Loads of fireworks, what a sight.

December heralds Santa Claus
Christmas goodies in all the stores.
Lots to eat, hearts full of cheer
Another one gone, Happy New Year.

***Carol Griffiths***

## THE LAST OF THE BRAVE

The anger of the soldiers turned to tears
as the shells rained over their heads
when the enemy approached, the air filled with fear
as friends lay wounded or dead

The awful smell of dead in the air
made most of them sick with sadness
each man who had gone, had someone who cares
as the enemy attack with madness

There was a time when comrades were talking
sharing rare moments with friends
now only the brave were barely walking
as most of their lives reached an end

The young ones unexpected to last so long
had exploded in a fit of fear
as the bombs landed and the sirens rang
no saviour was destined to appear

Their lives ending before beginning
their loved ones had to be told
a war with no reason that no one was winning
was leaving the bodies so cold

Gazing around, they searched in vain
searching for the hope that the last of the brave
would stand so strong and ease their pain
though victory was clear, the loss was grave

Now the ground they fought on is peaceful once again
thanks to the effort soldiers gave
they fought and died never in vain
we salute you the last of the brave

***David Wasley***

## Conversational Piece

As I moved around the tables
About my daily task
Collecting empty plates and glasses
'Is this all to life?' I ask
What makes it all worthwhile
What livens up my day
What really makes me smile
Is the things that people say.

Snippets of conversation
Tantalise my ears
'Has Betty really done a bunk?
It's bound to end in tears.'
Next time I pass to clear away
Things have moved along
I hear his mother's come to stay
And his name is John.

I shall never know what happened
I haven't got a hope
Snippets of conversation
It's like a never ending soap.
Intriguing, fleeting moments,
Confessions, tales of woe
Listening to all life's fragments
Boring . . . never, oh no!

***Carole M Pickworth***

## RAGING SEAS

Seagulls battling against the breeze
Swooping down to the choppy seas
Diving in and out of the waves
As the raging water engulfs the caves
Battering the rocks with a mighty roar
Each one louder than before
The spray is cascading over the bridge
Suspended across from ridge to ridge
Coastal paths eroding away
Causing the earth to fall and decay
Man cannot tame the power of the sea
As it gathers pace in its ferocity
When it has run its powerful race
It will slacken off the raging pace
Rolling back simultaneously
All is peace and tranquillity

***Marion Pollitt***

## The Old Barn

In all weathers here I stand,
Four square and enduring,
A testament to workmen's pride,
Cosy and alluring,

I must be so, as more than once,
In my long life enduring,
They've exclaimed, 'I must have that!'
And set about procuring,

Without success, so hard they tried,
Tenaciously enduring,
The Planning Officer's near contempt,
Enthusiasm souring,

The whims of folk who want to change,
My purpose all enduring,
To them I say, 'Just go away,
And get on with your touring!'

***Lois Ounssi***

## REFLECTION

Unfocused puddle,
Just as well, as he doesn't want to see his reflection.
Another night, nothing in sight,
But the rain and empty streets,
Hunched up to stay dry
Hidden to avoid prying eyes.
Glowing lights from shop displays,
Words start to blur in the haze.
Trying to think back to the last time he ate,
Not in hours, but a date.
So long ago, starting to lose track,
If only there was a way to turn the clock back.
Once he had it all,
Now it's just the clothes in which he'll fall.
But will it be tonight
That he could go down?
No time for a last confession,
As he ends up face first in his own reflection.

***Adam Davis***

## VIEW FROM A WHEELCHAIR

A bright sunny day, I'm out for a stroll
With Mum pushing my chair all's under control.
I enjoy the fresh air, the change of scene
Along the wide pavements I travel
*unseen.*

At least that's the way it seems to me
When they talk to my pilot and not to me.
'How is she today?' or 'How has she been?'
Why ask my nursemaid? If you are so keen

To know all about it, why not ask me
I've got a brain and feelings you see?
It hurts so much when you talk over my head,
It's only my legs and feet that are dead.

My mind is alive and so is my heart
I love to talk and to be a part
Of daily life, of the bustle, and care
Very deeply for people from here in my chair.

So next time we meet please talk to me,
We'll have a good chat and then you will see
That I'm a normal person who lives and loves
To say thanks for my life to the Lord above.

***Marion Holt***

## SUMMER SUN AND CAT

She sits there all day;
Lazily,
Watching the world go by,
wondering if today will be different
but not really caring.

A stretch and a yawn
is energy expired,
moving occasionally to follow the sun.
A static charge of fur
is a minor occurrence.

Ears twitch a shrug and then,
to her supposed master,
a feast an excuse not to kill;
then idly, rhythmically returns
to continue nothing and everything.

Eyes follow, a sudden blur
the chase ensues,
her tail caught,
trapped in a paradox or so we thought.
Enough is enough, never, always.

The day will end, her day begins.
Moon, stirs within, with senses sharp.
Ready just in case, needles and pins,
with danger lurking,
but secretly wishing . . . warmth.

Over and under, stillness.
To lie and think and dream
of battles gone and yet to come,
as dawn arrives.
Forever, summer sun and cat.

***Ged M Bretherton***

## THE WASTE

You took the life, from nature and me,
like in the forest, you cut down the tree.
It didn't matter, what the people said,
you let your power, go straight to your head.
You're building now, yet another way,
or so the politicians all seem to say.
Is it just another, quicker route,
For all those ambitions, in close pursuit.
What about all, the people's opinions,
who asked all, the millions.
Who gave you, the justified right,
to crush nature, out of sight.
You're not in a position, to now rebuild,
the beauty, we once called a field.
You ploughed away, all the earth,
taking the roots, of nature's birth.
Who gave you, the sole right,
with your diggers and all their might.
Your high finance plans, of the future
they should have just, removed the tutor.
He taught you, meanings all wrong,
he forgot to tell you, where you belong.
You shouldn't treat, the earth with contemption,
to spoil for profit, is the wrong temptation.
What about, giving us the choice,
what about listening, to the people's voice.
All these people, can't be wrong,
leave nature alone, where she belongs.
Hear our voices, we shout out loud,
of our beliefs, of which we are proud.
Now listen, to the general population,
or take notice, of a new generation.
There's nothing left now, any more
we didn't do this much damage, in the war . . .

***P T Swayne***

## IT'S THE HOLIDAYS

'Grandma, I can't find my new Vauxhall car
I buried it somewhere here.'
A desert of sand
versus two plastic spades,
while his brother with bucket
runs seaward; falls flat
on his face in a rockpool.

'Grandma I'm waiting to play crazy golf
You said we could do it today.'
An ocean of shorts
sand-filled socks, dirty pants
blocks the washing machine, and
I've promised his brother
a wildlife park visit.

'Grandma I don't go to bed until nine
and I really love chilli con carne.'
A wasteland of plates
from their tea blocks the sink.
In the bedroom young brother
snores gently, and dreams of
crab fishing tomorrow.

'Mummy, why couldn't we stay one more day?
I don't want to go home yet.'
A mountain of shells
fishing nets, plastic toys
fills the boot of the car and
I kiss him and brother
and long for oblivion!

***Tricia Gerrish***

## Golden Trumpets

My house is full of daffodils
Now that springtime is here,
They tell me winter time has gone
And summer is quite near.

There's daffodils for Mother's Day
A gift from Sunday School,
A pretty posy wrapped in foil
An annual golden rule.

There's daffodils left on the step
With a note so plain and clear,
To cheer me up, when I am down
From a friend, so dear.

There's daffodils from a neighbour
To help to bring me cheer.
The sun shone, as she gave me them
Making the gesture clear.

There's daffodils from relations
Picked from their garden bright,
So big, and strong, and healthy,
A really lovely sight.

But, daffodils look so lovely
Growing under a tree,
Their majestic faces reaching up
For everyone to see.

Daffodils dancing in the breeze
And growing at the wayside,
Don't pick them, and make them into a bunch,
Leave them, in their pride.

***Joan Smith***

## RESTLESS NIGHT

It's the end of another long hard day
enough to make your hair turn grey
But never mind, it's time for bed
just as well, 'cos you feel half dead.

Check the doors and windows too
Just the way you always do
Then climb the stairs one by one,
no energy left to run.

Now, the moment you've dreamed of for so long;
such bliss it must be wrong,
Snuggled up nice and warm
safe from outside's raging storm.

Hours later and still awake,
you need to sleep, for goodness sake!
But worrying thoughts invade your mind
and there's not a hope that you'll unwind.

So up you get and back downstairs
hoping a cuppa tea will chase your cares
But when it's brewed and in the cup
you're painfully aware the sun'll soon be up.

Sleepy now and much more calm
but you're right back where you began;
Climb the stairs and into bed
now too close to the hour we *all* dread!

This time no need for sheep
two minutes and you're fast asleep.
Then suddenly, what a shock
that noise - it's the damned alarm clock!

***Isabel Murray***

## Innocent Within

Look into a child's eyes
see the innocence within
but all too soon the innocence is gone
the child that was is destroyed
The shell which is left is the adult
with memories of happy and gleeful times
the adult becomes one of many
that special feeling has gone
like the childhoods of those who went before
when you grow up you lose the child within
memories linger dreams are shattered
life goes on but the adult in me
would rather be the child again
innocent eyes innocent soul
child and adult
to make you fell whole

***Karen Henderson***

## THE LOVE CHILD

I loved you from the start
No matter what they said
That loving feeling inside
Their poison put into my head.

I know the timing was not right
I know I was young and wild
But who were they to pass judgement?
You were mine, all mine, my *love child.*

Their silence they think my mind will change
Their offers of things more nice
Oh little one keep kicking deep inside
You're staying at any price.

Soon your new born cry was heard
So tiny meek and mild
A tiny person of my own
You're mine my darling *love child.*

Through years I've watched you grow
Words forgotten they pretend
But their loving comes too late now
Just you and me until the end.

So maybe our timing wasn't right
No matter how young and wild
No other love will ever come close
To ours, my only *love child.*

***Alison Birch***

## What a Wonderful Feeling

What a wonderful feeling
there's so much to see,
and so much to buy
before baby makes three.

What a wonderful feeling
what a wonderful joy,
will we have a girl
or will we have a boy?

What a wonderful feeling
this baby inside,
it fills me with love
and so much pride.

What a wonderful feeling
it must be,
having a little baby
as a part of me.

***Kirsty Louise Penfold***

## HURT

Walking, looking at the ground,
Looking up, looking all around.
Sitting on the bench staring at the wall,
Feeling the pain, the hurt, the anger, feeling so small.
As the tears of despair trickles down my fearful cheek,
I know that I am about to weep.
I feel like dirt,
Like dying.
Please I need guiding.
What things are running through my mind,
And all because I'm blind,
Blind of friendship.

***Karla Jaggers (11)***

## Grace

It is morning, yet darkness appears
With no light to highlight the loss of life
Yet they know.

Grasping the gravestone, she weeps,
Life and breath escape from her,
Both are difficult to replace.

She looks to the sky
The air is filled with peace
As the memory, released and free
Floats to the clouds.

***Claire Shrewsbury***

## BEFORE I DIE

Up goes the battle cry, please God don't let me die.
Bullets flying, men dying, shells falling.
Men calling out for help.
Hoping for life coping with death.
Blood seeping, loved ones weeping.
Fear in their eyes, pain in their hearts.
Marching forward one step at a time,
All in a line.
Going slowly at first, moving faster with each pace.
Who will win this deadly race?

One by one they fall.

Guns flashing, men dashing this way and that.
Bodies falling all around me, laying in a heap by my feet.
Every step they take, could this be the last one they make?
In the mud, with blood flowing like lake.

Friends laying where they fall.

Bayonet clashing, hope for peace dashing,
When will it end?
All this noise and hate!
Soldiers moving forward at a deadly stride.
I feel something hit my side
I think about God

I don't want to die.

As I lay on my back looking up to the sky
Thinking am I going to die?
With every breath I think will this be my last?
As I remember the past it goes by so fast.
If it will only slow down,

Time will be on my side.

My heart beating faster,
I don't think I can last much longer.
I feel no pain or anger as I close my eyes,
And forget the hate.
I thank God,

Before it's too late.

***Denis Joseph***

## My Wish For Mankind In A Troubled World

Love find's its way into our hearts
And life takes on a meaning new.
The every day cares, the hates, the fights
Seem, suddenly, to become so few.
This is because, as God once did,
We place a person, a cause, a duty
Above ourselves and, in doing so,
The world takes on a greater beauty.

Perhaps if we could capture and keep
This new-found, soul-searing flame alive
Throughout our lives, and let it burn, undying
How great a blaze would spread,
How many lives its warmth would feel,
How many breaches its fire would heal.

Then nations, peoples, black and white
Now haggling and fighting about their right
To live, according to their own plan,
Would stop and look back at the Master's plan,
To be filled with a need to share sorrows and joys,
To help create love in our young girls and boys.

By example, design, courage and truth
Set a goal, to be aimed for, by the world's restless youth.
To bring back the caring, the smiles and the grace
Which the Master intended for His human race.

***Maureen Joy Lynch***

## Treasured Memories

Like me do you remember
When the kids were young and small
Before they became people
And grew so very tall

When it was their birthdays
And they would sit down by your side
Wondering what there was for them
With eyes opened so wide.

When their eager little faces
Were so happy and aglow
They were not afraid to show their love
Anyone could know.

The barmy things they did
The words they couldn't say
I find it sad to know how soon
These things all fade away.

Christmas was the best of all
When they would all believe
Santa filled their stockings
Sometime on Christmas Eve.

I've had all of this happiness
Is it selfish for me to yearn
If only it were possible
For those treasures to return.

You may not have had these pleasures
Not everyone will do
But I think you may remember
When that little child was you.

***A Langley***

## VICTORY

It's not a dream it's Victory Day
The clouds of war have rolled away
Through a mist the future gleams
Full of promise, hopes and dreams
But first before we sing and cheer
Think who made this victory year
Those who fought so well and true
A nation's warmest thanks to you
Those who paid the highest price
We must not forget your sacrifice
Oh God we owe you everything
Remember this when peace bells ring.

***D H Reasbeck***

## Delights Of Yorkshire

Summertime walks in open spaces,
Market Weighton and Ripon races.
Knaresborough, Mother Shipton's well,
the river, birds, arched bridge and fell.

Valley Gardens, where people play,
in Harrogate, down by the stray.
Newmillar Dam, where birds are born,
and varying sounds that greet the dawn.

Wakefield Cathedral, with its spire,
with The Ridings for people, when they tire.
Cafés galore, and afternoon tea,
at Scarborough, and Bridlington by the sea.

Whitby, where Dracula came to rest,
Robin Hood's Bay, where seagulls nest.
Choppy seas and briny smells,
Cleethorpes and Filey's great hotels.

Ilkley Moor and Barnsley Chops,
Leeds and Sheffield, with their shops.
Meadowhall for shopping too,
York, where most things are on view.

Museums, parapets, and great stone gates,
and a beautiful Minster, for religious dates.
Pontefract and its liquorice cakes,
coalmines, textiles and historical dates.

Wetherby and Pontefract Races,
Doncaster and Selby's market places.
Pately Bridge deep down in a valley,
where often hikers come to rally.

Bradford and Halifax, Dewsbury too,
places, close by for you to view.
Yorkshire, famous for its dales,
open moors and howling gales.

***Andrew Dickson***

## MELIKA

My daughter who is seven
Came down to me from Heaven
She brought life to my eyes
And gave me a surprise
So loving with care
She simply . . . was there
Without the need, or the will
She comforted me still
The love we have for each other
Is greater than any other
Her beauty stands, inside out
With her, I never need to shout
She fills me with calm
For she holds so much charm
So clever with her words
Her attitudes never hurt
She holds all her worth
Since the day of her birth.

***Suzan Gumush***

## The Shadow

The shadow moves across the land
Hesitating, selecting, commanding
Once the choice is made, the chosen ones depart
Never to return.

Gone forever, but to where?
The answer hidden in the mist of time
Revealed only to those selected
Each in their turn.

The clock strikes the hour
An old life ends replaced by a new
The wheel turns full circle
Spring, summer, autumn, winter
The shadow impervious to seasons
Stalks the land, its search never ending.

Age meaningless, whether young or old
The dice once cast, the decision is final
Protestations to no avail, the shadow having beckoned,
Its icy mantle wraps around its choice
Is this the end, or a new beginning?

Oblivion, dust carried away on the wind
Only the shadow knows the answer
As it closes the book of time.

***W W Lund***

## STRONGEST

Looking out towards the polluted
sea
I could see determined young men and
women
Furiously swimming against the cutting
waves
Until some reached a breaking
point
And through sheer exhaustion succumbed and
drowned
Twenty five yards later many more
perished
Ten yards to the shore, five yards to
shore
and only a handful were
left
but now they were trying to drown each
other
The strongest one's pulled
through
and staggered to dry
land
Never looking back, they put on dry
clothes
and made a dash towards the
city.

***Patrick Miller***

## The Park

The hot sun beating down
Sanctuary sought in the park in town
Willows sway, branches sweep the ground
Like a dancer's dress rustling sound

The cropped grass springing underfoot
Couples entwine not caring a hoot
Children's carousel, slide and swings nearby
Fatigued mothers give a sigh.

Then the lonely people with no-one to care
Sit on the seats taking in the fresh air
Perhaps no-one talked to them that day
Unknowing others pass on their way.

Spoiled by vandals this park will go on
Drug users leave their litter, what a mess
This is the world of today
Joy to some many care less.

***Clare Whitaker***

## SUMMER

Soft white clouds drift high above the hill
Buttercups and daisies in the meadow still.
A skylark hovers overhead.
In the field, strawberries red.
Yellow roses scent the way, this summer's day,
Breathing in the sea, a minute's walk away.
On pebble shore, we talk.

Soft white clouds disperse for golden sun,
As fishermen bring in a tone
Of small, white fish on tidal turn.
They laugh and joke with one another,
As boy meets lover.
The salt air touches her hair
And seagulls spread their wings.

Soft white clouds come drifting back.
Ponies along the track.
Picnic baskets, tennis balls,
Father, to son calls
'Ice-cream cornets, fizzy drinks.'
The sun sinks
On kaleidoscope scenes
Of summer.

***Pauline Burton***

## Confined Optimism

Controlled. Distorted
The force of life breaking through
Untroubled. Limitless
Not to have to think:
to be able to react on impulse
to wander and stroll through the images
I so want to devour . . .
I am unable to taste such succumbing fruit
let my desires consume me
become my reality.

***Emma Scott-Smith***

## QUERY TO A FRIEND

Your education far surpasses mine,
You've smoked your cigarettes and drunk your wine.
But have you read the books I've read?
Have you laid awake, lonely in your bed?
Do the demons whisper in your ear
As the clock ticks on, dawn drawing near?
No sleep last night, no dreams, no peace
Just desolate spirits, torn and creased.
Fear of loneliness, fear of time
Passing me by, no reason, no rhyme.
Just a query to a friend, who will
Remember in the end?

***Lee Spencer***

## FLAMES

Patterns on pavement intertwining
Leaves, all shapes and colours binding -
Blending and lending a flame to the air -
Drying and dying and rustling there.

Leaves from the oak, and sycamore,
So beautiful living and dead even more
Looking so vibrant, and glowing as flames
Laughing children scattering in their games.

The golds and reds, yellow and amber,
Memories of autumn for all to remember
Leaving bare branches for snow soon to cover -
Warming the earth, with love for the mother.

The mother who cherished the seed;
Blown by the wind in its time of need
To the place where its roots could spread
Nourished with food from the bed.

The warmth of the earth, and the rain,
Swelling and filling the grain.
Many years will worry by, till the
Leaves from that seed, will fill the sky.

***P Morrill***

## Thoughts And Dreams

Dawn breaking, a new day.
The feeling of anticipation, come what may.
Majestic trees whispering to you.
Sunlight, reflecting on a lake, like a huge mirror,
Perfect and true.
Beautiful roses climbing up a wall,
Refreshed with the morning dew.
A secret garden with colours of every hue.
A place to dream and meditate, as the warm
sunshine spreads across the sky.
With time to smile, and time to sigh.
Strolling by the sea.
Watching the waves, as they reach the shore.
Seeing the children playing about,
Hearing them, as they jump and shout,
A quiet walk down a leafy lane.
Snowflakes falling against a windowpane.
A cosy fire with an inglenook,
A warming drink, and a good book.
The first daffodils heralding the spring,
The sound of church bells, as they ring,
A friendly chat, with a cup of tea.
Soothing music for company.
Thoughts and dreams to fill our days,
as each of us go our separate ways.

***Margaret J Robinson***

## I'M SURE TADPOLES BITE

'Watch out' said mum 'Be careful out there,'
'OK mum' as I fell on the stairs,
How proud I was, they were red and new,
Shiny rubber, shoe size two.

I called on Alan from over the road,
Big brother Alf answered, he was a toad,
Down to the pond, first cross the lane,
Fishing nets and buckets to carry our gains.

The weather was hot as we caught the tadpoles,
I twisted my ankle down a fox hole,
'Take off your welly and give it a rub,'
Alfie said kindly, but he was a grub.

I did as he said, Oh! What a mistake,
Alfie took it 'Don't throw it in the lake,'
It was worse than that he didn't throw it
He proceeded to pour the tadpoles in it

'Please don't do that, they're brand-new,'
'Shut your mouth, the other one too,'
'No!' I said but he made a fist,
He was bigger than me and he seldom missed.

I cried and sobbed and wailed at him,
It mattered little 'Put your feet in 'em,'
My right foot gingerly entered the welly,
Alf was creased up holding his belly.

The cold aspic jelly came over the brim,
As the tadpoles decided they wanted to swim,
To this day I hate all things about frogs,
But most of all I hate Alfie Boggs.

***John A Marsden***

## RECOLLECTION

It was twilight approaching dark
As I strolled leisurely in the park.
Children were there playing with a ball
Beneath a pine tree standing so tall.

Being young at heart I joined in their fun
Till exhausted, I could no longer run.
I sat to rest my weary legs
Beside an old gypsy woman making clothes pegs.

In the distance I heard a dog bark
Then the call of a nightingale or was it a lark.
This filled me with a great joy
For I'd heard it once before when I was a boy.

Aroused by the quietness of the night
I was all alone with no one in sight.
Had it all been as it did seem
Or was it all only a dream.

One thing for sure the older I grow
The answer to which I may never know.
Was it a nightingale or a lark
That I'd heard in the park.

***A D Tarr***

## NEVER TO KNOW A MOMENT OF LONELINESS

With him around me
With him in my life
I was never to know a moment of loneliness
I was always surrounded
I was over-populated by people
People who meant nothing
People who just lingered
Like a bad smell
'Faces we see, hearts we do not know'
Their faces were visible with smiles
Their hearts were hidden
Their hearts I could not see
Because I could not see
I did not know
If I did not know
I could not trust
A smile
That can deceive
So readily, so easily.

***Saiqa Parveen***

## Unsure

Who smiles
Behind her smile?

Why is she
Smiling now
At me?

Was I betrayed
In some dream,
Or lost
In reality?

Perhaps
She is smiling
Because of me.

***Barry Taylor***

## A Place For Me

As I stand there at the stile
I take a seat to stay awhile
to take in all that is around
sights of beauty and nature's sound
there is a magical morning haze,
the slight breeze creates the meadow to Mexican wave
the chatter of trees as the foliage chafes together
off the distant hill a waft of wild heather
there's the river with its own song
mesmerising, calming as it meanders along
cutting a sway through the hill
reaching and working the old water mill
birds flit from tree to tree
their song a chorus across the skies
heightened and lifted then down it dies
scents of wild flowers blankets the air
the sight on the horizon of a wild galloping mare
its mane flying and momentarily suspended in space
it's spooked by ghosts that run in its race
all nature's beauty is here in this place
and for a moment in time was *my own private place.*

***Amanda Keighley***

## Special Woman

Have you an ever-loving wife? A loyal one and true?
Though she be fifty years or more, she glistens like the dew.
Love, kindness, peace and faithfulness are just some of her assets -
just like a diamond, flashing light, from all its many facets.

Her voice she uses like a balm, like fragrant oil or grease -
to soothe life's mental aches and pains, so that you may have peace.
When problems rise she's by your side to back you to the hilt,
and stress and strain she does relieve that you may never wilt.

The smell of freshly cooking food that wafts around your chair,
the ever-ready pot of tea are pleasures that you share.
The polish on the furniture displays a woman's touch -
and flowers on the mantelpiece, these things you love so much.

And does your love grow stronger still as time goes swiftly by? -
then come my friend, rejoice with me for such a wife have I.

***Jonathan Bryant***

## A Winter's Night

Scary, staring icy moon
Casting her silvery spell
On the haunting scene.
Shining between spindle trees
That loom darkly,
Draped in swirling swathes of mist.

Our lunar sister, serenely shines
Accompanied by her celestial cousins,
Sparkling points of distant stars
Illuminate the frosty velvet sky.

The call of a lonely owl
Pierces the silence.
As he waits patiently
Spying a condemned, solitary mouse
Scrabbling in the undergrowth;
Swooping silently down
The predator seizes his quarry.
A desolate final squeal, proclaims
The sad demise of the tiny creature;

Hours pass, and the moon is eclipsed
Behind layers of nebulous cloud
Massing in the dawn sky,
Laden with their frozen cargo
Of winter's crystal foam.

Snowflakes float silently
Down to the dreamy earth,
Quilting the landscape
With a fabric of immaculate white.
Trees become ethereal sculptures
Their crystalline architecture
Lends an innocent quality
To their winter nakedness.

***Carole Morris***

## MOTHER

When I was small I needed you,
to love, protect and care.
To me you were the light of my day,
someone who always was there.

As I grew up it was strange to see
the changes in you it couldn't be.
Angry, drunk and always sad
Why did I have to be so bad?

Pleasing you was hard to do,
no matter how hard I tried.
I cleaned, cooked and went to school
but you never blinked an eye.

Instead you were cold, hard
and with a heart that's full of stone.
Oh please! Wake up and see the pain
of a child that's so alone.

I longed to see that glow in your face
that beautiful smile so full of grace.
With open arms I'm begging you,
to cuddle me, because I need you to.

I think of you every day
since you left and went away.
The awful shock was hard to bear
you went alone and left me there.

I made a promise to God above
to give my children lots of love.
To listen to them would be a start
and never ever break their heart.

I realise now it wasn't me,
you live your life in purgatory.
With a man that caused you misery
who broke your heart and made you flee.

Being a mother is so special to me
It's an endless bond for eternity.
With children who I'm proud to love
and I kept my promise to God above.

***Alison Head***

## TIME

Tick tock it's the sound of the clock and the time is passing by.
Every second, every minute and hour of each day time
passes on and very soon another day has gone.
We never really notice how quickly days go by,
only changes in the season can tell us why
without glancing at the clock - time is passing by.
Tick tock it's the sound of the clock our lives are passing by
and every second we grow older not noticing the time,
until one day we stop and say - can that really be the time.
Tick tock.

***Helen S Newey***

## ISN'T IT A LOVELY DAY

The sun, the wind, the snow, the fog, the rain.
These are all words that speak to us of weather.
They're almost like a musical refrain.
That we, the waiting chorus chant together.
'Isn't it a lovely day,'
Are the words we'd like to say.
The sky's so blue, the breeze so light
That being out is pure delight.
Unfortunately what's more true
And makes us take a different view:
Is that we get far too much rain
And stormy winds and gloomy days.
So usually we have to say
'What a nasty day today!'
But looking on the brighter side,
We can imagine far and wide,
That we are miles and miles away,
Perhaps in sunny Spain.
With lapping waves and azure skies,
Just being there, by the seaside.
With not a thought of cloud or rain
Then we can really truly say
'Isn't it a lovely day!'

***Rowena O'Mahony***

## Biscuit Blues

There's an open packed of coconut rings beside me on the floor;
I eat them to forget.
The packet's growing empty now and I'll have to buy some more;
Coconut rings have put me in debt.

***Michelle Power***

## Changing Times

Today I sit cosseted in earthly change
no flickering flame, white ashes doom.
Anaemic hands clasped, transparent
knuckles bare.
Striving in rumpled chair, vanity of youth suppressed.
Feline cradled warmth exploding in the crest of belly tissue
welcome cast, in-stroking gesture at my fingertips
sing your monotonous purr to me.
chiming wooden casket standing dust
encrusted in the corner.
Loud ticking distracts . . . momentarily
drift-back to cold reality.
How I wish I was furniture . . .
or am I?

***Frances Kennedy***

## THE BATTLE

The Scottish Jacobites and English Redcoats fought,
There was blood in sight but they carried on to fight,
There were bodies on the ground, lots of cries and sounds.
Some were proud, brave and nervous but all had hope that day.
The bagpipes and drums were playing
And the Jacobites and Redcoats were praying that they would win,
But the Redcoats won, it was a shame,
But the Jacobites were not to blame,
For it was flat ground!

***Rachel Angus***

## Costumes And Scenery

Not much has changed since time began
to further the immortal plan.
Has mankind seen its finest hour?
Can we not curb the waste of power?

Only the costumes and the scenery changed,
The plot to keep man's mind deranged
goes on to vex and bind his soul,
whilst powers contrive to gain control.

Conditioning and sly connection
would make believe life is perfection.
Whilst power-mad beings grab their shares,
poor starving souls, die unawares.

***S Whitehead***

## WIND WHISPERS

Motionless,
head laid on the window frame
she perches on the ledge,
her wavy coat
astir in the light breeze.

Eyes shut, nostrils flaring,
the wee black dog is lost
in a cosmic world of smell,
as she maps the varied scents,
wafting up the loch.

Her body has become all nose,
intensely involved
in the wide spaces beyond
the Loch Aber bird-hide.

I find myself dog watching,
not bird-watching.
My senses awaken to her pleasure,
and I hold my breath,
lest I disturb her concentration.

***Betty Tindal***

## King Of Rings

Henry VIII succeeded his father
The king a ruthless man money he would rather
A prince of the Renaissance
Saw war against France
Preferring castles jewels and vintage wine
Silver gold velvet tunics materials fine
His first wife Catherine of Aragon
Could not bear a son and was no paragon
Sir Thomas More and second wife Anne Boleyn
Were executed for what he thought a sin
Third wife Jane Seymour died giving birth
To Edward VI only son turned to grief and sadness not mirth
Henry's fourth wife Anne of Cleaves
For the 'Flanders Mare' a 'diplomatic union' there was reprieve
Divorced her to marry Catherine Howard his fifth wife
Two years later by execution took her life
His final and sixth wife Catherine Parr
Married and settled within renewed war
Between France and Scotland a tyrant at home
Content with her and didn't want to roam
Wealth and money had the king
Happiness wasn't always found in his wedding ring.

***Ann Copland***

## Tomorrow

We've all had our share of sorrow
Felt our share of pain
It was but yesterday we wept
Today we start again.

A new day dawns tomorrow
We can smile once more
For on the past we turn our back,
And open the future's door.

Tomorrow may be full of gladness
Free from pain and fear
For who would dream of sorrow
Until the sorrow's here?

And if the days unfold themselves
As barren as before
Why, then, there's still tomorrow
To dream about once more!

***Julia Ann Davis***

## SMILE

To catch a smile and feel it seep to the heart!
To sense a flutter in your step and know recall!

To come full circle and soar like dreams,
As that smile lingers in your mind,

No thought of time only the heart that has thrown the smile,
In appreciation or happiness, in friendship or love,

Yet the reason has no function! The smile!
The reflection of peace of a moment's relaxation, from life.

Was for that brief moment a joy!

***Douglas Bonthron***

## GLOBAL WARNING

Today there is a lot of talk about global warning,
But nobody takes it seriously or don't they care,
About what is happening to our green planet,
Or the warnings and dangers that are there.

The seas are rising as ice caps melt,
Cliffs and shores being gradually washed away,
With high tides water is creeping further inland,
In spite of the valiant efforts to keep it at bay.

Gone are the winters on Christmas cards,
With bright sun shining on crisp white snow.
Now it is rain, gales and mud,
We have lost our four seasons of long ago.

Tornadoes and hurricanes crush things in their way,
Thunderstorms add to the terror,
People will one day, when it is too late,
Remember they had the choice of their error.

Rainforests are being quickly thinned out,
With no thought of the future, just profit today.
Forest fires rage out of control
Destroying environment, wildlife in its way.

We know the reason, people don't care.
Deadly fumes from cars drift out,
The reactors and factories add to pollution
It's the future generation we must think about.

***Margery English***

## WINTER TIME

In all the coldness
of the stark white snow
as the morning air
carries the breezing blow
the flurries of snowflakes
blind my eyes
with the passion of winter's
unpredictable surprise
cold white daylight
over the Earth's mantle ring
compressing Earth to give
rise to uplifting spring.

***Lynne Heather West***

## EMILY JANE

Parsnip Heath lay beneath great fortresses of cloud
Emily Jane dressed as rain wearing her deathly shroud
Walks daintily, rather faintly, screaming out her sins
Her words are heard by passing birds
But who, like metal tins, care nothing for the sins:
They keep on flying south
They care nothing for the sins or words
From such a mouth.

***Shaun Hillen***

## The Visit

Look at me! Look at me!
This is what you see.
Don't look away - askance, unseeing
It's me! It's me!

Look at me! Look at me!
Suspended in time I may be.
Don't look away in dismay
Help me! Help me!

Look at me! Look at me!
Out of touch with reality.
Don't look away, stay for a day
It's me! It's me!

***V Magrs***

## THE NEIGHBOURS FROM HELL

In the place where we dwell
We have the awful neighbours from Hell.
Loud music is played all day and all night
Screaming and shouting ends up in a fight.
The garden's a tip, debris all around,
The walls are so thin you hear every sound.
A tinkle of glass a crash of a pan
I'm so fed up with it honest I am.
We have thought of moving,
To somewhere new,
But that's what these neighbours
Want you to do.
We're staying put, just hope it will cease
Our life may one day
Be Peace Perfect Peace.

***S A Buckingham***

## CYRIL VC

On the 30th of March in 1944,
With success still some way off in the Second World War,
From his base at Burn, near Selby, into the dark night,
A young Christian, Cyril, and his pals, flew off to fight.

Though the lad knew well the Bible says 'Thou shalt not kill,'
And that from the bombing much innocent blood must spill,
Had he, and his mates, sat back and done nothing at all,
Jackboots, by then, could well have been marching down Whitehall.

Hitler had to be stopped, and the best way Cyril knew
Was by piloting a Halifax and, with his crew,
Risking life and limb above the Ruhr and elsewhere,
By taking the battle right into the Nazi lair.

Hence the night in question when a huge attacking force
Of almost eight hundred aircraft from these shores set course,
Lancasters and Halifaxs, for Nuremberg bound,
However, for many, disaster waits to be found.

For Cyril too it strikes, with enemy fighter fire,
Leaving his 'kite' in a situation that is dire;
Three vital crew bail out in the resulting mess,
Leaking tanks; guns, intercom and one engine US.

But he carries on to the target where his bomb-load
Is dropped, then whilst struggling home his prowess really showed;
With no-one to navigate, and fuel being lost fast,
Somehow he's able to reach the English coast, at last.

Here, missing balloons and friendly fire, those tanks run dry,
On what but skill and luck can the pilot now rely;
Fighting to keep control, he finds all his speed is gone
As, into a coalmine yard, his bomber lumbers on.

From the wreckage Cyril's three crew mates left walk away,
For this though, at twenty-two, his life has had to pay;
Yet the Bible says too what greater love can there be
Than such heroism, which also won a VC.

***Richard Beeson***

## KEEP SMILING

First thing in the morning
What's better than a smile
It makes one so charming
It's well worth your while.

The lilies and roses
They smile in the sunlight
The sheep and the horses
What a beautiful sight.

The mother and baby
With love smile and joy
The proudest of lady
No matter, girl or boy.

The birds are all nesting
Where the hatching is bright
When the sun is smiling
And the chicks come to light.

A smile make the beauty
On everyone's face
So keep smiling happy
And be thankful for grace.

***B Phillips***

## TITANIC

That fateful night
Whispering ocean star-filled night
Beauty in steel motionless
Position with grace prepares descent
Destination a darkened resting place
Edwardian souls young and old
Perish in confusion that echoes
Survivors few cast silent prayers
Over lost ones never spared.

***Alan Jones***

## The Dead Poet

Lost in time with nowhere to go.
Slowly dying like leaves on a tree.
With no more to give and nothing to say.
Trembling while looking for words.
The poet left each poem she gave,
With a message between the lines.
Put there specially for you.
To hope you will understand the story
That she has left behind.
As the poet can give no more.

***Amanda Hillbeck***

## An Educated Scarecrow

Cheap talk, cheap words,
vanity is like an educated scarecrow,
his talk was cheap, and he fooled her with his lies.

She mapped out his motives,
and turned over his cards of deceit.
She watched him from her bedroom window,
as he lit up a cigarette in his car.

How could you love through a web of deceit,
it was like a game of chess,
she had the winning move,
but she let him win, just for the sake of winning,
he already cheated her out of her heart.

She didn't know how he did it,
but he knew how to fan the flames of her heart,
they burned for one another,
she couldn't make the killing move,
she knew she could, but the flame burned too bright.

***K J Herbert***

## Taking Time To Care

There is a man across the way,
Who smiles and waves most every day.
When he needs me I go to the shop,
and when I want a cuppa over I pop.
He lost his wife and a year has passed,
I hope our friendship will always last.
To make him feel wanted is enough for me,
and through that window, that smile I see.
It doesn't take long to bring someone joy,
and not just forget them like a worn out toy.
We should all take the time to find a friend,
Then perhaps all their broken hearts we could mend.

***Mandy Jayne Moon***

## SUMMER OF '41

A Spitfire! Is it? No it ain't, can't really see, it's much too faint
My mates and me out for a stroll, the bombs, they fill our streets
with holes
They smash the buildings, cause great fires, they haven't touched
St Paul's big spires
The sirens start, we're filled with fear, when will it stop,
six months? a year?
The planes come almost every night, to fill our homes with gelignite
They said they'd never go for towns, make people rush
in dressing gowns
They run in panic all around, and head straight for the underground,
Where safety lies, with friends and neighbours, lots of *cups of char*
to savour
The plane's much closer now! We hide, in case the pilot that's inside,
Is not our friend, and fires his gun, and kills another father's son
He's really close, what speed! What pace! Cor! We can even
see his face
He's looking, searching, causing pain, we see the *black cross*
on the plane
*German!* My mate Johnny cries, a strange expression fills his eyes
I wonder, 'Is he really bad,' I wonder 'Did *he* kill my dad'
I wonder if he woke today, and wished somebody's life away
Does he have children, his to love, do they fear planes that fly above
I don't suppose they have to care, our planes don't kill them over there
We only shoot at trucks and trains, we don't kill people, not *our* planes
But now he's gone, gee all that fuss, he wanted just to frighten us
We laugh, we joke, we think war's rotten, but just for now
it's all forgotten
We run, we jump, we shout, we play, the war can come *another day.*

***P W Spencer***

## WHY DON'T MY CHILDREN LOVE ME

Why don't my children love me?
Why don't my children care?
They never come to see me
To see how much I care

Why don't my children love me?
As I truly love them all
And even after many years
I still miss and love them all

Why don't my children love me?
True sickness grief and pain
I truly felt so lonely then
Why won't they come again?

Why don't my children love me?
Oh how I wish they would
For life is so very short
And I love them like I should

Why don't my children love me?
Oh what I wouldn't give
To put my arms around them all
I have so much love to give

So all your lovely children
Who come from miles apart
Please think about your mother
Who loves you from the heart.

***Janet Brown***

## Modern Medicine

I was feeling ill
So I took a pill.
That made me worse -
Hence this verse.

I took another pill
And still felt ill.
So I threw them out.
Now I'm up and about.

***Helen Cronin***

## Growing Pains

Susie, she is very small, never seems to grow at all,
Unlike brother Timothy, who is as tall as he can be.
In between there's sister Pearl, who is quite average for a girl.
Each child frets about their shape,
Oh please grow up for heaven's sake.
Growing pains can be a strain,
I remember feeling just the same.
The horrors of their spots and pimples,
they even complain about their dimples.
The nice thing is, they will survive,
and later smile with knowing eyes.
When like the links in life's great chain,
once again experience teenage pain.

***Veronica Black***

## An Englishman's Home

Castles in the air
Are all the homes that some may own
Shop doorways are their palaces,
The wind their telephone
Dustbins are the kitchens
That provide their daily bread
Begging for a living,
But they're moved along instead

Charitable shelters
On the increase do their bit
Whilst politicians
In the House of Commons warmly sit
Homelessness, contagion
That has spread across the land
And governmental policies
Don't give a helping hand

The cardboard box, a feature
Of our modern city life
Containing folk surviving
On the edge of each day's knife
So common that they blend
Into the bustle of the street
They invite you to their table,
Won't you come and take a seat?

***Kim Montia***

## Sometimes

Sometimes I am happy
 because of love's illusions.

Sometimes I am sad
 because my soul despairs.

Sometimes I am tearful
 because my heart weeps.

Sometimes I am hopeful
 because my dream is near.

Sometimes I am tired
 because of daily grind.

Sometimes I am grumpy
 because of problems anew.

Sometimes I am lustful
 because I love you.

***Stephanie Bones***

## Poem For A Princess

Diana, Princess of Wales,
To support charities she never fails.
England's rose,
In which people's hearts this shows.

Princes William and Harry,
And Dodi who you were about to marry.
You were the Queen of everyone's heart,
And from there you will never part.

***Laura Sage (13)***

## BILL

That day we saw you was a shock
But God cannot turn back the clock
You offered us a piece of cake
And told us of all the plans you'd make
You told us of your exciting trip
On life you then still had a grip
There was so much you wanted to say
But time ran out that particular day
But now dear Bill release the pain
A new life soon will start again
A baby we've all been waiting for
It's now time to unlock that door
You're with us in every thought
A lesson to us all you've taught
And that's to be strong and brave and kind
Rest now dear Bill with peace of mind.

***F E Cove***

## DIANA

The whole world is crying
every colour and creed,
for a princess who cared
about people in need.

Tears of sadness
some, of regret
for a woman we loved
and will never forget.
She gave us hope right
from the start
will always remain
queen of our hearts.
Like a beautiful flower
nipped in the bud
we'd all bring her back
if only we could.
How could it happen
did she have to die?
Only, God in his wisdom
can tell us why.

***Anne Scrimshaw***

## Beauty - To Paint

How I wish that I could paint
The things that I can see
The colour of a rosebud
The beauty of a tree
The crash of waves upon a rock
The lake so clear and blue
The mountains - dark forbidding
The flowers of different hues
I can write it down on paper
Words come easy to describe
What I can see and feel and touch
What I see with my eyes
The colours in a murmuring stream
The plumage of a bird
I wish I could use paints and brush
Instead of using words.

***Lydia Barnett***

## FOLLOWING YOUR DREAMS

Go for your dreams
Achieve your goals
Fulfil the wonder
Or you'll never know
Feel the success
Grasp the fame
Live life to the fullest
Never take the blame
Collect all the riches
Attend every do
Speak of the wisdom
And how it belongs to you
Pardon yourself
Have no regrets
Quote on your life
Never feel ashamed
You've got what you wanted
Now you've others to save.

***Danielle Turner***

## Love

*(Dedicated to Michael with love)*

Love is the seed planted in my heart
from you my love will never part
A love so strong, a love so true
my heart has chosen you

Love is comfort through the tears
reassurance through the fears
tenderness on a cold dark night
you are my guide, a shining light

Love is a dream that has come true
all that is beauty I see in you
you gave me hope when my heart had none
this life I have been given has only just begun

Love is this endless need for you
I pray that you will love me too
like an ever-burning fire
you are my heart's desire

Love is everything I can't replace
captured in your smiling face
I see my children in your eyes
their little smiles I visualise

Love is growing old with you
and when we've lived our whole lives through
you will look into my eyes
and see the love that never dies

Love is never having to part
your love will never leave my heart
life without you - so meaningless and hollow
wherever you may go I will surely follow

Love is all that life is worth
it stretches far beyond this Earth
and when it is our time to leave
we shall not cry, we shall not grieve.

Love is Holy, good and true
and there in Heaven I'll find you
we'll meet again and be together
our love will live again - forever.

***Rachel Johnston***

## Reasons

Pity was not the feeling I had when I returned
It was more a pang of remorse because I had taken so long
Childhood memories of the place were mixed
Large, friendly, in a time warp.

My visit was for a different reason
A new-found friendship and its cultivation
A 'sense' of deja vu was not apparent
Although I knew the old haunts well.

Sadness possessed me when the old ties were sought
Some had changed, many remained unaltered
The decision to go back was out of my hands
Regret was not what I felt.

To retrace one's steps is to lay the ghost
Painful thoughts surface only to be repressed
I reviewed the place with new eyes
Experience of the years an aid.

Large, friendly, 'in a time warp' still rang true
The reunion of old thoughts with new emotions
Was cleansing, refreshing and vital
For our recent association to thrive.

***M M Kirkham***

## FIREMOON

Like the passion I feel,
Like the true love I know now,
And my heart's alliance to my twin soul,
One thought, one path, one destination.

The burning moon, sovereign star,
Like the fire in me, speeding my heart,
The ascending, capturing spirit of desire,
Enthralling, possession of inspired warmth,
Shifting and sliding, sheltering white angel.

Guardian of the night's heaven,
Guardian to our nights, in rest,
Peaceful in our days, long and fulfilling,
To our eternity in love.

***Stuart A Brown***

## ON GLANCING THROUGH A HOLIDAY GUIDE

I notice that the guide-books always dwell
Upon the glamour and forget the smell.
I hate to mention it, but sun-drenched ports
Lose their romance when drains are out of sorts
And sanitation is just left to fate;
And please don't think me too indelicate
If I should warn you that there's not a hope
That natives use a certain toilet soap!

***Eileen Bales***

## GOD'S FAMILY

We are not half-hearted in our belief
Of *Our Father* in *Heaven*
For we know whole-heartedly that it's true,
Do join us, you're welcome,
Then thro' the *Love* of *His Son,* our *Saviour,*
You will get to know *Him* too.

To know *The Lord* our *God*
Is a miracle in itself
As it will change your life forever
For *He* is with you every minute,
Yes, ten thousand and eighty in just one week
Now isn't that the *Blessing*
Which all mankind should seek?

With the *Priest* whom we hold in the highest esteem
Standing in here on Earth as host,
            *'God's Go-Between'*
You will become one of the family of
            our *Father* above
And find not only friendship
But also that of great worth
Which is so rare in the world of today
*Love, caring love.*

***Emily Hodson***

## I Wish

I wish Lady Luck would smile on me,
so a win I'd have on the Lottery.
I'd spend and spend with such glee
buying gifts for my family

Who would love to feel secure
in receiving things money can procure.
Yet I would rather have good health
than a bulging purse . . . though
I wish.

Owning things which we all treasure
only brings a 'fleeting' pleasure,
but if my lifestyle I could enhance
I will continue to take a chance
and put my hopes on Lady Luck,
I wish.

***M Wakefield***

## Spring

Spring is sprung the saying goes
Though what is meant no one knows
A cocktail of dreams which drives the mind
And gives us hope for all mankind
The birth of everything began
Was made aware with just one man
The slow awakening of the Earth
Was given us by the virgin birth
The blossoms with their fragrance sweet
Epitomises spring.

***M Tickle***

## Growing Old

Whatever you do, don't grow old
It makes you feel so weary
With aches and pains everywhere
How can we all feel cheery.

There's pains in backs, and wobbly knees
With indigestion growing
Some cannot hear, and some not see
And yet life keeps a'flowing.

We grumble and moan, all no use
We are told 'You're wearing out'
But we cannot get replacements
So we have to sit and shout.

There's stainless steel joints and false teeth
Linctus and tablets galore
We have blood tests for this and that
Sometimes blood pressure will soar.

There's contact lenses and glasses
And hearing aids by the score
Whatever you do, don't grow old
Unless you get a rebore.

***Edith Buckeridge***

## Snow In Scotland

Bob Johnson, the weatherman,
Encourages us all to enjoy
All seasons.
Deep snow and ice can be dangerous,
But it can be fun.

Sliding and sledging,
Bringing smiles to our faces.
Building snowmen in fields, gardens
And streets,
Brings us laughter, cold hands
And cold feet.

***Kenneth Mood***

## HEAVEN CALLED FOR OUR ANGEL

'Slowly' each second will tick away,
To soothe the shock, we felt that sad day,
When the world, heard of Princess Diana's fate,
'Why' was this accident to happen, 'This day'.
Our Princess, Diana, so violently she died,
Many nationals, prayed, and cried.
All her life, compassion she asked, of one to another,
Yet a broken heart, she was driven to suffer,
Two sons, they would be a comfort, to their mother,
When her husband Prince, forsook her, for another.
Friendship, she sought, from a friend,
They would never know, both their lives would end.
Her 'happiness' was never to be,
'Rest in peace Diana' till eternity . . .

***Brian Marshall***

## PAST AND PRESENT

'Tis many years since I walked this shore
I thought of the years that had gone before.
A laughing pair that ran on the beach
Carefree and young, no sorrow could reach.
But 'twas not to be, for far out at sea
My love said farewell.
Eternally.
But now as before, I walked on the shore
Hand held by another young man.
A tear in my eye, oh . . . mem'ry can't lie
The child said 'Are you crying gran?' . . .
'Oh no, my dear 'tis the wind I fear
That has made my eyes seem wet'
'You run so fast!' (I live in the past)
And my heart will never forget . . .

***Ivy Cawood***

## For Armistice Sunday

I saw a man - he was going to war,
I said 'Why are you going?' - He said 'I am not sure.'
But I love my country, my king and my friends,
I wonder if we'll all be here when the fighting ends?

Every village and hamlet, every city and town,
Sent both men and women to fight for the crown;
To bring peace and security back to our land,
To show to the world, it is for freedom we stand.

The sound of the guns - the roar of the planes,
We bear it all to break tyranny's chains;
For freedom a gain, to us a great loss,
Our bravest are remembered by a name on a cross.

I saw that man again at the end of the war,
His face was all scarred and his feet were so sore;
He had marched over desert and mountain and fell,
And for years has survived in a slow lingering hell.

But he was one who had made it safe home to his wife,
To his children and kindred to claim peace out of strife;
And now he is at peace with those long battles won,
With his home and country free - and his duty well done!

***Douglas Peet***

## ISLAND OF DREAMS

In those beautiful islands of my dreams
The fresh cool waters flow in gentle streams
How large are those beautiful grapes upon the vines
Their sweet juices are pure like God's Heavenly wings.

Those awakening meadows are daily awashed with the dew
The wonderful sunrises are like a crown of jewels.
Those clear currents flow sedately in those silver streams
In those beautiful islands of my refreshing dreams.

Where every night the sky wears its black velvet gown
And the pale moon wears its wonderful silver crown.
That's where my body lies so peacefully in my dreams
When I see those tiny deers drinking from those flowing streams.

I will tell how I find this Heavenly island of my dreams
When my unclean body is washed by those living streams.
How faultless are the large fruit hanging upon those trees
When I was always young and my dreams are given free.

***J F Grainger***

## LIFE IN THE YEAR 9791

One night I woke in the year 9791
In a paradise human colony
On the Uranus moon of Desdemona
In the glorious 98th century!

There were no disabled or sick
Everybody was rich, well and happy
The people were living forever
Through nonageing bioimmortality

No governments or councils
To tell people what to do
No need for taxes or licences
So nobody was blue

Lots of toys for the kids you see
Lots of channels on the 3D interactivision
A domed city of 300 levels
All in clean perfect condition

Suddenly I woke to the bad world today
To see Tony Blair outside No 10 with glee
But governments must be gone by 2000
If my future dream is to come true see.

***H G Griffiths***

## LIMITED EDITION

Hills and valleys,
Rivers and streams,
Fill the pages of the book,
Of the countryside's dreams.

Inhabitants of the woodland,
- Forest and field,
In each paragraph own a place,
And have the right to be.

Warmed by the sunlight,
Tormented - by the rain,
Till the snowfalls of winter
Form a bookmark - on each and every page.

Owning a lifestyle of their own,
With no need of others -
To tell them - when, how or why,
Only the pleasure - of forever living,
- In the freedom -
Of God's beautiful countryside.

***Bakewell Burt***

## THE TRUCK STOP 2000

They used to call them Truck Stops
Joe's or the Greasy Fork the trucker's heaven who knows
The place for a wash and brush-up and to pass the time away
The place for a big greasy fry-up eggs bacon beans and . . .?
A place to park, a place to sleep, a place for all their needs
A place that's dying out now unfortunately to say
Now you get the motorway service stations
The Little this or Beef that with fries and all that stuff
The beefburger and chip joint or a posh place for a full four course
But give me The Old Greasy Fork and the old caravan
At the side of the road The Bacon Butty stop
Where you get a pint of tea or coffee not something in a cup
The truckers drive in old blue overalls
Not pin-striped suits and the mobile phone yuppies
The trucker on the old CB trying to find his route
10/43 traffic hold-up or 10/55 drunk driver
10/36 what's the time and there's more
10/73s and 10/88s love and kisses to you all
So 10/10 till we do it again
I'm down and clear and out of here
Hand in my pocket and off like a rocket down the old A1.

***Donald Jay***

## HUMP PHERY

There was a large animal that lived in the desert and was rather
down in the dumps.
You see his friends laughed at him for having large humps.
His friends did tease, and he grumbled and growled and said if you
please. I'm supposed to have these humps and chumps you see I don't
care what you say they are helpful on a very hot day, you see I'm
not a fish or a bird or a cat or a mammal.
I'm Humphrey the dromedary camel.

***James R B McCurdie***

## Imaginary Friend

Throughout one's early childhood, you were never quite alone
A friend was there beside you, someone to call your own
If ever you were lonely, your broken heart he'd mend
To all intents and purposes, he was an imaginary friend.

Call on him any time, any hour in the week
If you chatted to him, you never heard him speak
No one else could see him, yet always at your side
Playing most exciting games, like run away and hide.
Sweets and toys you used to share, playing on the park
Always there to comfort you, even in the dark
And when the games were over, the day was at its end
You would curl in bed beside him, your imaginary friend.

As you grew up, he went away, without a wave goodbye
I hear he plays with other kids, it makes you want to cry.
And though you sometimes miss him, thanks to him you send
For always being there for you, your imaginary friend . . .

***GIG***

## Sensations

I touch the tree's worldly bark,
Its roughness is quite harsh,
Listen to the song of the lamenting lark,
See the butterflies, over the marsh.

A new sensation fills my senses,
It makes me feel quite heady,
I see a deer escape, over fences,
It's time to end! No it's not ready.

The woody herbs and grasses,
Give off their worldly hue,
Pungent, acrid in their masses,
Nothing further they need to do.

Musk and jasmine filled my being,
The sun caressed my eyes
Even closed they were ever seeing,
To me it held no lies.

Insects, fleeting and buzzing around,
Drinking off the flowers,
Animals, insects scurrying underground,
I could sit and watch for hours.

Cracking, creaking, slowing down,
The light it is now fading,
In its magic I could drown,
Tangent auras my senses raiding.

***Gail Susan Halstead***

## True Friends

Friends are very far and few, that's why I found a friend in you.
You're like my brother like no other, through thick and thin
you were always in.
From sweets to toys to girls to noise all those things were both
our choice.
From beginners to sinners we were always winners,
Friends are very far and few, that's why I found a friend in you.

***Timothy Webster***

## WIND

You can hear it, feel it when it's there
Whistling through trees and blowing your hair
Biting into your skin it makes you shiver
As it whisks up spray from the lakes and river.

Sometimes it's rough and very, very strong
Other times gentle as it glides along
It can be frightening as it throws things about
Then calming and pleasant on a summer's day out

Lying in bed it howls through the night
Keeping us awake with its eerie might
This invisible force is both friend and foe
And you're never sure when it will show

It helps nature to get on its way
Blowing seeds and creatures around all day
So you never know when the wind will be there
But one thing's guaranteed you will always get your fair share.

***D J Blackburn***

## THOUGHTS OF YOU

I work my day with thoughts of you
I sleep at night and dream of you
I abide my time until I hear from you
My heart aches for you
I want to spend my time with you
Time waits for nobody
Time can make one bitter
Time can make one sad
Our time should be full of happiness
Cosy and warm - let me hold you
I love you from the bottom of my heart.

***Mia Ryan***

## INFORMATION

We hope you have enjoyed reading this book - and that you will continue to enjoy it in the coming years.

If you like reading and writing poetry drop us a line, or give us a call, and we'll send you a free information pack.

Write to :-